DISCOVERIN
MEDITERRANEAN
DIET

A Complete Guide for Beginners. Get Started on Your Wellness Journey with Quick, Easy, Healthy Recipes and Expert Nutrition Advice.

Alice Auster

TABLE OF CONTENTS

INTRODUCTION

Welcome to "Flavors of the Sun: A Delicious Journey through the Mediterranean Diet," where we embark on a gastronomic adventure that will transport you to the sun-kissed shores of the Mediterranean. With its vibrant colors, tantalizing aromas, and mouthwatering flavors, the Mediterranean diet offers a holistic approach to healthy living and exquisite culinary experiences.

In this book, we invite you to discover the secrets of one of the world's most renowned and scientifically proven dietary patterns. Embracing the Mediterranean way of eating is not just about shedding unwanted pounds but also about embracing a lifestyle that nourishes both body and soul. From the olive groves of Greece to the vineyards of Italy, and the coastal villages of Spain, we will explore the diverse flavors, ingredients, and traditions that make this diet so exceptional.

Prepare to savor an array of fresh fruits and vegetables, fragrant herbs and spices, heart-healthy fats, whole grains, and lean proteins. Learn how to make olive oil the cornerstone of your kitchen, how to appreciate the simplicity of a Mediterranean salad, and how to embrace the joy of communal dining. Discover the remarkable health benefits, including reduced risk of heart disease, diabetes, and cognitive decline, that have made the Mediterranean diet a gold standard in nutritional science.

Whether you are a seasoned chef or a novice in the kitchen, "Flavors of the Sun" provides you with a wide range of delicious recipes, meal plans, and practical tips to help you effortlessly adopt this lifestyle. Get ready to tantalize your taste buds, nurture your body, and embark on a culinary journey that celebrates the Mediterranean's rich heritage and the pleasure of good food shared with loved ones. So, grab your apron, invite your family and friends, and let's dive into the vibrant world of the Mediterranean diet!

CHAPTER 1 : BREAKFAST

TROPICAL SUNRISE CHIA SMOOTHIE BOWL

This vibrant bowl is quick to prepare, making it an ideal choice for breakfast or a satisfying snack. It serves 2 people and can be whipped up in just 10 minutes.

Ingredients:

- 1 cup of frozen mangoes
- ½ cup of fresh mangoes
- 2 tablespoons of sliced almonds
- 2 teaspoons of chia seeds
- 1 ½ tablespoons of flavored protein powder
- 1 teaspoon of unsweetened maple syrup (or alternative sweetener)
- 2 tablespoons of unsalted cashew butter
- ¼ cup of coconut granola
- ½ cup of unsweetened coconut milk
- 1 teaspoon of ground nutmeg

Instructions:

1. Place the frozen mangoes, protein powder, cashew butter, maple syrup (or alternative sweetener), and coconut milk in a blender. Blend until you achieve a smooth consistency.
2. Divide the mixture equally between two serving bowls.
3. Sprinkle sliced almonds, chia seeds, coconut granola, and ground nutmeg over each bowl for added texture and flavor.
4. Serve and savor the tropical goodness of your Tropical Sunrise Chia Smoothie Bowl!

Nutritional Information per Serving:

Calories: 370 Total Fat: 17g Saturated Fat: 2.5g Carbohydrates: 32g Sugar: 16g Fiber: 7g Protein: 25g

BERRY BLISS SMOOTHIE BOWL

Preparation time: 10 minutes
Servings: 2

Ingredients:

- 1 frozen banana
- 1 cup frozen mixed berries (blueberries, raspberries, strawberries)
- 1/2 cup unsweetened almond milk
- 1/4 cup plain Greek yogurt
- 2 tablespoons chia seeds
- 1 tablespoon agave nectar (or honey as a substitute)
- 1/4 teaspoon vanilla extract
- Toppings of your choice, such as fresh berries, sliced bananas, granola, and almond butter

Instructions:

1. In a blender, combine the frozen banana, frozen mixed berries, almond milk, Greek yogurt, chia seeds, agave nectar (or honey), and vanilla extract. Blend until the mixture becomes smooth and creamy.
2. Pour the blended mixture into serving bowls.
3. Decorate the smoothie bowls with your favorite toppings, such as fresh berries, sliced bananas, granola, and almond butter.
4. Serve immediately and savor the delightful Berry Bliss Smoothie Bowl!

Nutritional Information per Serving:

Calories: 320 Total Fat: 10g Saturated Fat: 1g Carbohydrates: 51g Sugar: 29g Fiber: 10g Protein: 11g

BLISSFUL BERRY MEDLEY SMOOTHIE BOWL

Preparation time: 10 minutes
Servings: 2

Ingredients:

- 1 frozen banana
- 1 cup frozen mixed berries (strawberries, raspberries, blueberries)
- 1/2 cup unsweetened almond milk
- 1/4 cup plain Greek yogurt
- 2 tablespoons chia seeds
- 1 tablespoon agave nectar (or honey)
- 1/4 teaspoon vanilla extract
- Toppings of your choice, such as sliced bananas, fresh berries, granola, and almond butter

Instructions:

1. In a blender, combine the frozen banana, frozen mixed berries, almond milk, Greek yogurt, chia seeds, agave nectar (or honey), and vanilla extract. Blend until the mixture reaches a smooth consistency.
2. Pour the blended mixture into a bowl.
3. Garnish your smoothie bowl with toppings of your choice, such as sliced bananas, fresh berries, granola, and almond butter.
4. Serve immediately and indulge in the blissful flavors of the Berry Medley Smoothie Bowl!

Nutritional Information per Serving:

Calories: 300 Total Fat: 9g Saturated Fat: 1g Carbohydrates: 50g Sugar: 28g Fiber: 10g Protein: 10g

TROPICAL PARADISE SMOOTHIE BOWL

Preparation time: 10 minutes
Servings: 2

Ingredients:

- 1 large ripe mango (peeled and sliced)
- ½ frozen banana
- ¼ cup coconut milk
- 2 tablespoons almond butter

Instructions:

1. In a blender, combine the peeled and sliced mango, frozen banana, coconut milk, and almond butter. Blend on low speed until the mixture is smooth and creamy.
2. Pour the smoothie into a bowl.
3. Sprinkle your desired toppings, such as sliced almonds, chia seeds, granola, or fresh fruit, over the smoothie bowl.
4. Indulge in the refreshing and nourishing delight of the Tropical Paradise Smoothie Bowl!

Nutritional Information Per Serving (1 bowl):

Calories: 210 Total Fat: 13g Saturated Fat: 6g Carbohydrate: 22g Sugar: 16g Fiber: 4g Protein: 7g

BOUNTIFUL VEGGIE EGG BAKE

Prep time: 10 minutes
Servings: 2

Ingredients:

- 1 tablespoon olive oil
- 2 cloves garlic, minced
- ½ red bell pepper, diced
- ½ onion, diced
- 1 cup broccoli florets
- 4 large eggs

Instructions:

1. Preheat the oven to 400 degrees Fahrenheit. Grease a baking sheet with olive oil or cooking spray and set it aside.
2. In a medium bowl, combine the minced garlic, diced bell pepper, diced onion, and broccoli florets.
3. Spread the vegetable mixture evenly on the prepared baking sheet, creating a single layer.
4. Bake the vegetables for 10 minutes or until they have slightly softened.
5. Move the vegetables to one side of the pan, making space for the eggs.
6. Carefully crack the eggs onto the empty side of the pan.
7. Return the baking sheet to the oven and bake for an additional 10 minutes or until the eggs are cooked to your desired doneness.
8. Serve the Bountiful Veggie Egg Bake warm and enjoy!

Nutritional Information Per Serving (1 serving):

Calories: 137 Total Fat: 8g Saturated Fat: 2g Carbohydrate: 8g Sugar: 3g Fiber: 3g Protein: 9g

GOLDEN GLOW SMOOTHIE

Total Time: 10 minutes
Servings: 2

Ingredients:

- 2 cups fresh spinach leaves
- 1 frozen banana
- 1/2 cup frozen pineapple chunks
- 1 teaspoon ground turmeric
- 1 teaspoon grated ginger
- 1/2 cup unsweetened almond milk
- 1/2 cup plain Greek yogurt
- 1 tablespoon honey

Instructions:

1. In a blender, combine the fresh spinach leaves, frozen banana, frozen pineapple chunks, ground turmeric, grated ginger, almond milk, Greek yogurt, and honey.
2. Blend on high speed until all the ingredients are thoroughly combined, and the smoothie has a smooth and creamy texture.
3. Pour the smoothie into two glasses.
4. Serve the refreshing Golden Glow Smoothie immediately.

Nutritional Information Per Serving:

Calories: 145 Total Fat: 2g Saturated Fat: 0g Carbohydrate: 28g Sugar: 17g Fiber: 3g Protein: 7g

MEDITERRANEAN MORNING BRUSCHETTA

Prep time: 5 minutes

Servings: 1 serving

Ingredients:

- 2 slices whole grain bread
- 2 tablespoons hummus
- 1/4 avocado, sliced
- 1 small tomato, sliced
- 2-3 Kalamata olives, sliced
- 1 tablespoon crumbled feta cheese
- 1 teaspoon extra-virgin olive oil
- Salt and pepper, to taste

Instructions:

1. Toast the slices of bread until they turn golden brown.
2. Spread 1 tablespoon of hummus evenly on each slice of toast.
3. Arrange the sliced avocado and tomato on top of the hummus.
4. Sprinkle the Kalamata olives and crumbled feta cheese over the avocado and tomato.
5. Drizzle the bruschetta with extra-virgin olive oil.
6. Season with salt and pepper according to your taste preferences.
7. Serve and savor the delightful flavors of your Mediterranean Morning Bruschetta!

Nutritional Information Per Serving:

Calories: 280 Total Fat: 14g Saturated Fat: 3g Carbohydrate: 31g Sugar: 4g Fiber: 9g Protein: 9g

GREEN POWER BREAKFAST SALAD

Servings: 4
Total Time: 20 minutes

Ingredients:

- 4 cups mixed greens
- 4 soft-boiled eggs
- 1 avocado, sliced
- 1 small cucumber, sliced
- 1 small tomato, diced
- 2 tablespoons chopped fresh parsley
- 2 tablespoons lemon juice
- 1 tablespoon extra-virgin olive oil
- Salt and pepper, to taste

Instructions:

1. Wash and dry the mixed greens, then divide them among four plates.
2. Peel the soft-boiled eggs and slice them in half. Arrange two halves on each plate.
3. Add the sliced avocado, cucumber, and diced tomato on top of the greens.
4. Sprinkle the chopped fresh parsley over the salad.
5. In a small bowl, whisk together the lemon juice, extra-virgin olive oil, salt, and pepper. Drizzle the dressing over the salads.
6. Serve the Green Power Breakfast Salad immediately and enjoy the fresh and nutritious start to your day!

Nutritional Information Per Serving:

Calories: 220 Total Fat: 17g Saturated Fat: 3.5g Carbohydrate: 9g Fiber: 5g Sugar: 2g Protein: 10g

MEDITERRANEAN GARDEN OMELETTE

Total Time: 10 minutes
Servings: 1

Ingredients:

- 3 large eggs
- 1/2 cup cherry tomatoes, halved
- 1/4 cup chopped fresh spinach
- 2 tablespoons crumbled feta cheese
- 1 tablespoon chopped fresh parsley
- Salt and black pepper, to taste
- 1 tablespoon olive oil

Instructions:

1. In a small mixing bowl, beat the eggs with a pinch of salt and black pepper.
2. Heat the olive oil in a non-stick frying pan over medium-high heat.
3. Add the cherry tomatoes to the pan and sauté for 1-2 minutes until they start to soften.
4. Add the chopped spinach to the pan and sauté for another minute until it wilts.
5. Pour the beaten eggs into the pan, ensuring they cover the sautéed vegetables evenly.
6. Sprinkle the crumbled feta cheese and chopped parsley over the top of the omelette.
7. Reduce the heat to medium-low and cook the omelette for 3-4 minutes or until the eggs are fully set.
8. Carefully fold the omelette in half using a spatula, and then slide it onto a plate.
9. Serve the Mediterranean Garden Omelette hot, accompanied by some whole wheat toast or pita bread on the side. Enjoy your flavorful and nutritious meal!

Nutritional Information Per Serving:

Calories: 325 Total Fat: 24g Saturated Fat: 7g Carbohydrate: 8g Fiber: 2g Sugar: 4g Protein: 20g

CREAMY AVOCADO AND FETA SCRAMBLED EGGS

Total Time: 10 minutes

Servings: 2

Ingredients:

- 4 eggs
- 1 ripe avocado, mashed
- 2 tablespoons crumbled feta cheese
- 2 tablespoons chopped fresh parsley
- Salt and pepper, to taste
- 2 tablespoons olive oil

Instructions:

1. Crack the eggs into a bowl and whisk them together.
2. In a separate bowl, mash the avocado with a fork until it turns creamy.
3. Heat the olive oil in a non-stick pan over medium heat.
4. Pour the beaten eggs into the pan and let them cook for a few seconds until they begin to set.
5. Using a spatula, occasionally stir the eggs until they reach your desired level of doneness.
6. Add the mashed avocado to the pan and stir until it is well combined with the eggs.
7. Sprinkle the crumbled feta cheese and chopped parsley over the eggs, and season with salt and pepper to taste.
8. Serve the creamy Avocado and Feta Scrambled Eggs hot and savor the delightful flavors!

Nutritional Information Per Serving:

Calories: 318 Total Fat: 28g Saturated Fat: 6g Carbohydrates: 6g Fiber: 4g Protein: 13g

CREAMY CHEDDAR SCRAMBLED EGGS

Total Time: 10 minutes
Servings: 2

Ingredients:

- 4 eggs
- 2 tablespoons milk
- 1 tablespoon butter
- 1/4 cup shredded cheddar cheese
- Salt and pepper, to taste

Instructions:

1. In a bowl, crack the eggs and add milk, salt, and pepper. Whisk the mixture until the eggs are well beaten.
2. Melt the butter in a non-stick pan over medium heat.
3. Pour the egg mixture into the pan and stir with a spatula.
4. Cook the eggs for 2-3 minutes, stirring occasionally, until they start to set.
5. Sprinkle the shredded cheddar cheese over the eggs and continue stirring until the cheese has melted and the eggs are fully cooked.
6. Serve the creamy cheddar scrambled eggs hot and savor the delightful cheesiness.

Nutritional Information per Serving (serves 2):

Calories: 250 Total Fat: 20g Saturated Fat: 9g Total Carbohydrates: 2g Protein: 15g

SPINACH AND FETA FRITTERS

Total Time: 20 minutes
Servings: 4 fritters (2 servings)

Ingredients:

- 2 cups fresh spinach leaves, chopped
- 1/2 cup crumbled feta cheese
- 1/4 cup chopped scallions
- 1/4 cup all-purpose flour
- 1/4 cup bread crumbs
- 1 egg, beaten
- 1/4 teaspoon garlic powder
- 1/4 teaspoon salt
- 1/8 teaspoon black pepper
- 2 tablespoons olive oil

Instructions:

1. In a large mixing bowl, combine the chopped spinach, crumbled feta cheese, and chopped scallions.
2. Add the flour, bread crumbs, beaten egg, garlic powder, salt, and black pepper to the bowl. Stir until all the ingredients are well combined.
3. Heat the olive oil in a non-stick pan over medium heat.
4. Using a spoon, scoop the fritter mixture onto the pan and flatten each fritter with the back of the spoon.
5. Cook each side of the fritters for about 2-3 minutes or until they turn golden brown.
6. Serve the spinach and feta fritters hot and savor their deliciousness.

Nutritional Information per Serving (4 fritters):

Calories: 220 Total Fat: 14g Saturated Fat: 4g Sugars: 1g Protein: 8g Total Carbohydrates: 15g

SCRAMBLED EGG AND VEGGIE TACOS

Preparation Time: 15 minutes Servings: 4 tacos (2 servings)

Ingredients:

- 4 small whole wheat tortillas
- 4 large eggs
- 1/4 cup diced onion
- 1/4 cup diced bell pepper
- 1/4 cup diced tomato
- 1/4 cup shredded cheddar cheese
- 1 tablespoon olive oil
- Salt and pepper, to taste

Instructions:

1. Heat the olive oil in a large skillet over medium heat. Add the diced onion and bell pepper and cook for 3-4 minutes, until they start to soften.
2. Add the diced tomato to the skillet and stir to combine. Cook for an additional 2-3 minutes, until the tomato is heated through.
3. Crack the eggs into the skillet and scramble them with the veggies. Cook until the eggs are set and no longer runny, about 3-4 minutes.
4. Warm the tortillas in the microwave or a dry skillet.
5. To assemble the tacos, spoon some of the egg and veggie mixture onto a tortilla and sprinkle with shredded cheese. Fold the tortilla in half.
6. Repeat the process for the remaining tortillas and filling.
7. Serve the tacos hot and enjoy!

Nutritional information per serving (1 taco):

Calories: 186 Fat: 10g Carbohydrates: 15g Protein: 11g Fiber: 3g Sugar: 2g

BACON AND CHEDDAR BREAKFAST POTATO CAKES

Preparation Time: 15 minutes Cooking Time: 15 minutes Servings: 4

Ingredients:

- 2 large potatoes, peeled and grated
- 4 slices bacon, cooked and crumbled
- 1/2 cup shredded cheddar cheese
- 1/4 cup all-purpose flour
- 1 egg, beaten
- Salt and pepper, to taste
- 2 tablespoons vegetable oil, for frying
- 4 large eggs, cooked to your preference

Instructions:

1. In a large mixing bowl, combine the grated potatoes, crumbled bacon, shredded cheddar cheese, all-purpose flour, beaten egg, salt, and pepper. Mix everything together until well combined.
2. Heat the vegetable oil in a large skillet over medium-high heat. Once the oil is hot, use a spoon or cookie scoop to drop the potato mixture into the skillet, using about 2 tablespoons per cake. Flatten the mixture slightly with a spatula.
3. Cook the potato cakes for 3-4 minutes on each side, until golden brown and crispy. Once cooked, transfer the cakes to a plate lined with paper towels to drain any excess oil.
4. While the potato cakes are cooking, cook the large eggs in a separate skillet according to your preference.
5. Once the potato cakes and eggs are cooked, serve the potato cakes topped with a cooked egg and garnish with chopped fresh herbs or a dollop of sour cream, if desired.
6. Enjoy these delicious bacon and cheddar breakfast potato cakes!

Nutritional Information Per Serving:

Calories: 385 Total Fat: 27g Saturated Fat: 9g Carbohydrates: 20g Fiber: 2g Sugar: 1g Protein: 15g

SAVORY VEGETABLE AND GOAT CHEESE SCRAMBLE

Preparation Time: 20 minutes
Servings: 2

Ingredients:

- 4 large eggs
- 2 tablespoons milk or cream
- 2 tablespoons butter
- 1/2 cup diced bell peppers
- 1/2 cup sliced mushrooms
- 1/4 cup chopped red onion
- 1/4 cup crumbled goat cheese
- Salt and pepper, to taste
- Chopped fresh herbs, such as parsley or chives, for garnish

Instructions:

1. In a small mixing bowl, whisk together the eggs and milk or cream until well combined.
2. Melt the butter in a large skillet over medium heat. Once the butter is melted, add the diced bell peppers, sliced mushrooms, and chopped red onion. Cook for 5-6 minutes, stirring occasionally, until the vegetables are softened.
3. Add the egg mixture to the skillet with the vegetables. Use a spatula to stir the eggs and vegetables together until the eggs are cooked to your preference.
4. Once the eggs are cooked, sprinkle the crumbled goat cheese over the top. Season with salt and pepper, to taste.
5. Divide the scramble evenly between two plates. Garnish with chopped fresh herbs, if desired.
6. Enjoy this delicious vegetable and goat cheese scramble for a satisfying breakfast or brunch!

Nutritional Information Per Serving:

Calories: 322 Total Fat: 26g Saturated Fat: 12g Carbohydrates: 7g Fiber: 2g Sugar: 4g Protein: 15g

CHAPTER 2 : LUNCH

CHICKPEA AND OLIVE SALAD

Total Time: 20 minutes
Servings: 4

Ingredients:

- 2 cans of chickpeas, drained and rinsed
- 1/2 cup sliced black olives
- 1/2 cup sliced Kalamata olives
- 1/2 cup diced red onion
- 1/2 cup diced cucumber
- 1/2 cup crumbled feta cheese
- 1/4 cup chopped fresh parsley
- 1/4 cup olive oil
- 2 tablespoons lemon juice
- 1 clove garlic, minced
- Salt and pepper, to taste

Instructions:

1. In a large mixing bowl, combine the chickpeas, sliced black olives, sliced Kalamata olives, diced red onion, diced cucumber, crumbled feta cheese, and chopped fresh parsley. Mix everything together until well combined.
2. In a separate small mixing bowl, whisk together the olive oil, lemon juice, minced garlic, salt, and pepper until well combined.
3. Pour the dressing over the chickpea mixture and stir until everything is well coated.
4. Divide the chickpea and olive salad between four plates and serve immediately.
5. Enjoy this refreshing and flavorful chickpea and olive salad as a healthy and satisfying meal!

Nutritional Information Per Serving:

Calories: 378 Total Fat: 23g Saturated Fat: 6g Carbohydrates: 31g Fiber: 10g Sugar: 4g Protein: 13g

BLACK BEAN & MANGO SALAD

Total Time: 10 minutes

Servings: 4

Ingredients:

- 2 cups cooked black beans, rinsed and drained
- 1 mango, peeled, pitted, and diced
- 1/2 red onion, minced
- 2 tablespoons fresh cilantro, chopped
- 2 tablespoons lime juice
- 1/4 teaspoon chili powder
- Salt and pepper, to taste

Instructions:

1. In a medium bowl, combine the cooked black beans, diced mango, minced red onion, and chopped cilantro.
2. In a small separate bowl, whisk together the lime juice, chili powder, salt, and pepper to create the dressing.
3. Pour the dressing over the black bean and mango mixture in the bowl.
4. Gently toss the salad to coat the ingredients evenly with the dressing.
5. Serve the black bean and mango salad chilled or at room temperature.
6. Enjoy this refreshing and nutritious salad!

Nutritional Information Per Serving (1 bowl):

Calories: 201 Total Fat: 3g Saturated Fat: 0g Carbohydrates: 33g Sugar: 11g Fiber: 10g Protein: 11g

QUINOA AND BLACK BEAN SALAD

Total Time: 25 minutes
Servings: 4

Ingredients:

- 1 cup quinoa, rinsed
- 2 cups water
- 1 can black beans, drained and rinsed
- 1 red bell pepper, diced
- 1 yellow bell pepper, diced
- 1/2 red onion, diced
- 1/2 cup chopped fresh cilantro
- 1/4 cup olive oil
- 2 tablespoons lime juice
- 1 teaspoon ground cumin
- Salt and pepper, to taste

Instructions:

1. In a medium-sized saucepan, bring the quinoa and water to a boil. Reduce the heat to low, cover the saucepan, and simmer for 15-20 minutes until the quinoa is tender and the water has been absorbed. Fluff the quinoa with a fork and let it cool.
2. In a large mixing bowl, combine the cooked quinoa, black beans, diced red and yellow bell peppers, diced red onion, and chopped fresh cilantro. Mix everything together until well combined.
3. In a separate small mixing bowl, whisk together the olive oil, lime juice, ground cumin, salt, and pepper until well combined.
4. Pour the dressing over the quinoa mixture and stir until everything is well coated.
5. Divide the salad between four plates and serve immediately. Enjoy this flavorful and nutritious quinoa and black bean salad!

Nutritional Information Per Serving:

Calories: 388 Total Fat: 16g Saturated Fat: 2g Carbohydrates: 49g Fiber: 14g Sugar: 4g Protein: 14g

FRESH CUCUMBER AND TOMATO SALAD

Total Time: 10 minutes
Servings: 4

Ingredients:

- 2 large cucumbers, sliced
- 2 large tomatoes, chopped
- 1/2 red onion, thinly sliced
- 1/4 cup chopped fresh parsley
- 2 tablespoons olive oil
- 2 tablespoons red wine vinegar
- Salt and pepper, to taste

Instructions:

1. In a large mixing bowl, combine the sliced cucumbers, chopped tomatoes, thinly sliced red onion, and chopped fresh parsley. Mix everything together until well combined.
2. In a separate small mixing bowl, whisk together the olive oil, red wine vinegar, salt, and pepper until well combined.
3. Pour the dressing over the cucumber and tomato mixture and stir until everything is well coated.
4. Serve the salad immediately, or chill in the refrigerator for 30 minutes to allow the flavors to meld.
5. Enjoy this refreshing and vibrant cucumber and tomato salad!

Nutritional Information Per Serving:

Calories: 83 Total Fat: 6g Saturated Fat: 1g Carbohydrates: 7g Fiber: 2g Sugar: 4g Protein: 2g

THYME-ROASTED TOMATOES WITH FETA

Total Time: 25 minutes
Servings: 4

Ingredients:

- 2 pints cherry tomatoes
- 2 tablespoons olive oil
- 1 tablespoon fresh thyme leaves
- Salt and pepper, to taste
- 1/4 cup crumbled feta cheese

Instructions:

1. Preheat the oven to 400°F (200°C).
2. Spread the cherry tomatoes on a baking sheet lined with parchment paper.
3. Drizzle the olive oil over the tomatoes, and sprinkle the fresh thyme leaves, salt, and pepper on top.
4. Toss the tomatoes to coat them evenly with the oil and seasonings.
5. Roast the tomatoes in the preheated oven for 20-25 minutes until they are tender and blistered.
6. Remove the tomatoes from the oven and let them cool for a few minutes.
7. Transfer the roasted tomatoes to a serving dish and sprinkle the crumbled feta cheese on top.
8. Serve the thyme-roasted tomatoes with feta immediately, allowing the warm tomatoes to contrast with the cool cheese.
9. Enjoy these flavorful and aromatic roasted tomatoes with the delightful addition of feta cheese!

Nutritional Information Per Serving:

Calories: 95 Total Fat: 7g Saturated Fat: 2g Carbohydrates: 7g Fiber: 2g Sugar: 5g Protein: 3g

MEDITERRANEAN GARDEN SALAD

Total Time: 10 minutes
Servings: 4

Ingredients:

- 4 cups mixed greens 1/2 cup cherry tomatoes, halved
- 1/2 cup cucumber, sliced
- 1/4 cup red onion, thinly sliced
- 1/4 cup Kalamata olives, pitted
- 1/4 cup crumbled feta cheese
- 1/4 cup chopped fresh parsley
- 2 tablespoons lemon juice
- 1 tablespoon extra-virgin olive oil
- 1 garlic clove, minced
- Salt and freshly cracked black pepper, to taste

Instructions:

1. In a large bowl, combine the mixed greens, cherry tomatoes, cucumber, red onion, Kalamata olives, feta cheese, and chopped fresh parsley.
2. In a small bowl, whisk together the lemon juice, olive oil, minced garlic, salt, and pepper to make the dressing.
3. Drizzle the dressing over the salad and toss gently to combine, ensuring all the ingredients are coated.
4. Serve the Mediterranean garden salad immediately as a refreshing and healthy side dish or light lunch.

Nutritional Information Per Serving:

Calories: 150 Total Fat: 11g Saturated Fat: 3g Carbohydrate: 8g Sugar: 3g Fiber: 3g Protein: 5g

ROASTED CHICKEN AND SWEET POTATO SALAD

Total Time: 35 minutes

Servings: 4

Ingredients:

- 2 medium sweet potatoes, peeled and diced
- 2 boneless, skinless chicken breasts, cooked and diced
- 1 red bell pepper, diced
- 1/2 red onion, diced
- 1/4 cup chopped fresh parsley
- 2 tablespoons olive oil
- 2 tablespoons apple cider vinegar
- 1 teaspoon honey
- 1 teaspoon Dijon mustard
- Salt and black pepper, to taste

Instructions:

1. Preheat the oven to 400°F (200°C).
2. Place the diced sweet potatoes on a baking sheet and drizzle with 1 tablespoon of olive oil. Season with salt and black pepper to taste. Roast for 20-25 minutes, or until the sweet potatoes are tender and lightly browned.
3. In a large mixing bowl, combine the roasted sweet potatoes, diced chicken, red bell pepper, red onion, and chopped parsley.
4. In a small mixing bowl, whisk together the remaining 1 tablespoon of olive oil, apple cider vinegar, honey, Dijon mustard, salt, and black pepper.
5. Pour the dressing over the salad and toss well to combine, ensuring all ingredients are coated.
6. Serve the roasted chicken and sweet potato salad immediately or refrigerate for later.

Nutritional Information Per Serving:

Calories: 350 Total Fat: 12g Saturated Fat: 2g Carbohydrates: 30g Sugar: 10g Fiber: 5g Protein: 30g

SPICY SHRIMP AND AVOCADO QUINOA BOWL

Total Time: 30 minutes
Servings: 2

Ingredients:

- 1/2 cup quinoa
- 1 cup water
- 1/2 teaspoon salt
- 1/4 teaspoon black pepper
- 1/4 teaspoon garlic powder
- 1/2 pound shrimp, peeled and deveined
- 1 tablespoon olive oil
- 1/2 teaspoon chili powder
- 1/4 teaspoon cumin
- 1 avocado, sliced
- 1/2 cup cherry tomatoes, halved
- 1/4 cup red onion, diced
- 1/4 cup fresh cilantro, chopped
- 1 lime, juiced

Instructions:

1. Rinse the quinoa in a fine mesh strainer and place it in a saucepan with water and salt. Bring to a boil, then reduce the heat to low, cover, and simmer for 15 minutes. Remove from heat and let it sit for 5 minutes before fluffing with a fork.
2. In a small bowl, combine salt, black pepper, and garlic powder. Add the shrimp and toss to coat.
3. Heat olive oil in a skillet over medium-high heat. Add the seasoned shrimp and sprinkle with chili powder and cumin. Cook for 3-4 minutes, or until the shrimp is cooked through and slightly pink.
4. In a large bowl, combine the cooked quinoa, cooked shrimp, avocado slices, cherry tomatoes, red onion, cilantro, and lime juice. Gently toss to combine.
5. Serve the spicy shrimp and avocado quinoa bowl immediately and enjoy!

Nutritional Information per Serving:

Calories: 365 Total Fat: 15g Saturated Fat: 2g Carbohydrates: 37g Fiber: 10g Protein: 26g

ROASTED PEACH AND AVOCADO SALAD WITH CARAMELIZED ONIONS

Total Time: 25 minutes
Servings: 2

Ingredients:

- 2 ripe peaches, sliced
- 1 avocado, diced
- 1 red onion, sliced
- 2 cups mixed greens
- 1/4 cup crumbled feta cheese
- 2 tbsp. balsamic vinegar
- 2 tbsp. olive oil
- 1 tsp. honey
- Salt and pepper to taste

How to make:

1. Preheat the oven to 375°F. Line a baking sheet with parchment paper and place the sliced peaches on it. Drizzle with olive oil and season with salt and pepper. Roast for 15 minutes until tender and slightly caramelized.
2. While the peaches are roasting, heat 1 tablespoon of olive oil in a pan over medium-high heat. Add the sliced onions and cook until they are caramelized and soft, stirring occasionally.
3. In a small bowl, whisk together the balsamic vinegar, olive oil, honey, salt, and pepper.
4. In a large bowl, add the mixed greens, diced avocado, and crumbled feta cheese.
5. Once the peaches and onions are cooked, add them to the large bowl. Drizzle the dressing over the top and toss to combine.
6. Serve the roasted peach and avocado salad with caramelized onions immediately and enjoy!

Nutritional Information per Serving:

Calories: 285 Total Fat: 18g Saturated Fat: 4g Carbohydrates: 29g Sugar: 19g Fiber: 8g Protein: 6g

COCONUT LIME QUINOA SALAD

Total Time: 20 minutes
Servings: 4

Ingredients:

- 1 cup quinoa, rinsed
- 2 cups water
- 1/2 cup unsweetened shredded coconut
- 1/4 cup fresh lime juice
- 2 tablespoons extra-virgin olive oil
- 1 tablespoon honey
- 1/4 cup chopped fresh cilantro
- 1/4 cup chopped red bell pepper
- 1/4 cup diced cucumber
- 1/4 cup sliced scallions
- Salt and pepper, to taste

Instructions:

1. In a medium saucepan, bring the quinoa and water to a boil. Reduce the heat to low, cover, and simmer for 15 minutes, or until the quinoa is tender and the water is absorbed. Remove from heat and let it sit for 5 minutes. Fluff with a fork.
2. In a dry skillet over medium heat, toast the shredded coconut until lightly golden, stirring frequently. Remove from heat and set aside.
3. In a small bowl, whisk together the lime juice, olive oil, honey, salt, and pepper.
4. In a large bowl, combine the cooked quinoa, toasted coconut, chopped cilantro, red bell pepper, diced cucumber, and sliced scallions.
5. Pour the dressing over the quinoa mixture and toss to coat evenly.
6. Serve the coconut lime quinoa salad chilled or at room temperature.

Nutritional Information per Serving:

Calories: 240 Total Fat: 10g Saturated Fat: 4g Carbohydrates: 34g Fiber: 4g Sugar: 6g Protein: 5g

CHEESY HERB-ROASTED POTATOES

Total Time: 35 minutes

Servings: 4

Ingredients:

- 2 pounds baby potatoes, halved
- 1/4 cup olive oil
- 2 tablespoons fresh rosemary, chopped
- 2 tablespoons fresh thyme, chopped
- 3 cloves garlic, minced
- Salt and pepper, to taste
- 1/4 cup grated Parmesan cheese

Instructions:

1. Preheat the oven to 400°F (200°C).
2. In a large mixing bowl, combine the halved potatoes, olive oil, chopped rosemary, chopped thyme, minced garlic, salt, and pepper. Toss well to coat the potatoes evenly with the herb mixture.
3. Transfer the coated potatoes to a baking sheet, arranging them in a single layer.
4. Roast the potatoes in the preheated oven for 25-30 minutes, or until they turn golden brown and develop a crispy exterior while remaining tender on the inside.
5. Remove the baking sheet from the oven and sprinkle the grated Parmesan cheese over the roasted potatoes.
6. Return the baking sheet to the oven and continue baking for an additional 2-3 minutes, or until the cheese has melted and becomes bubbly.
7. Serve the cheesy herb-roasted potatoes hot and savor their delightful flavors.

Nutritional Information per Serving:

Calories: 212 Total Fat: 9g Saturated Fat: 1g Carbohydrates: 30g Fiber: 3g Sugar: 2g Protein: 3g

CREAMY ROASTED EGGPLANT DIP

Total Time: 1 hour
Servings: 4

Ingredients:

- 2 medium-sized eggplants
- 2 cloves garlic, minced
- 1/4 cup tahini
- 3 tablespoons lemon juice
- 2 tablespoons extra-virgin olive oil
- Salt, to taste
- Fresh parsley, for garnish (optional)

Instructions:

1. Preheat the oven to 400°F (200°C).
2. Place the eggplants on a baking sheet and prick them all over with a fork.
3. Roast the eggplants in the preheated oven for 40 to 50 minutes, or until they are tender and the skin becomes wrinkly.
4. Remove the eggplants from the oven and let them cool.
5. Once cooled, slice the eggplants in half lengthwise and scoop out the flesh into a bowl, discarding the skin.
6. Mash the roasted eggplant flesh with a fork or blend it in a food processor until smooth.
7. Add the minced garlic, tahini, lemon juice, olive oil, and salt to the roasted eggplant and mix well.
8. Taste the dip and adjust the seasoning as desired.
9. Transfer the creamy roasted eggplant dip to a serving bowl and garnish with fresh parsley, if desired.
10. Serve the dip with pita bread, crackers, or vegetables for dipping.

Nutritional Information per Serving:

Calories: 102 Total Fat: 9g Saturated Fat: 1g Total Carbohydrates: 6g Sugars: 2g Protein: 2g

PROTEIN-PACKED TURKEY AND QUINOA BOWL

Total Time: 30 minutes
Servings: 4

Ingredients:

- 1 cup quinoa, rinsed
- 2 cups water
- 1/2 tsp salt
- 2 tbsp olive oil
- 1 small onion, diced
- 1 red bell pepper, diced
- 2 cloves garlic, minced
- 1/2 tsp smoked paprika
- 1/2 tsp ground cumin
- 1/2 tsp ground coriander
- 1/4 tsp cayenne pepper (optional)
- 1 lb ground turkey
- 1 can black beans, drained and rinsed
- Juice of 1 lime
- Salt and pepper, to taste
- Chopped fresh cilantro, for garnish

Instructions:

1. In a medium pot, bring the quinoa, water, and salt to a boil. Reduce the heat to low, cover, and simmer for 15-20 minutes, or until the water has been absorbed and the quinoa is tender.Meanwhile, heat the olive oil in a large skillet over medium-high heat. Add the onion and bell pepper and cook for 5-7 minutes, or until softened.
2. Add the garlic, smoked paprika, cumin, coriander, and cayenne (if using) to the skillet and cook for 1 minute more, or until fragrant.
3. Add the ground turkey to the skillet and cook, breaking it up with a wooden spoon, until browned and cooked through.

4. Stir in the black beans and lime juice, and season with salt and pepper to taste. Cook for an additional 2-3 minutes to heat through.
5. To serve, spoon the cooked quinoa into bowls and top with the flavorful turkey mixture. Garnish with fresh cilantro, if desired.

Nutritional Information per Serving:

Calories: 480 Total Fat: 18g Saturated Fat: 3g Carbohydrates: 47g Fiber: 10g Sugar: 3g Protein: 35g

TEX-MEX BLACK BEAN SALAD

Total time: 30 minutes
Servings: 4

Ingredients:

- 1 can black beans, drained and rinsed
- 1 red bell pepper, diced
- 1 green bell pepper, diced
- 1 small red onion, diced
- 1/2 cup chopped fresh cilantro
- 1/2 cup crumbled queso fresco cheese
- 1/4 cup extra-virgin olive oil
- 2 tablespoons lime juice
- 2 cloves garlic, minced
- 1 teaspoon ground cumin
- Salt and pepper, to taste

Directions:

1. In a large bowl, combine black beans, red bell pepper, green bell pepper, red onion, cilantro, and queso fresco cheese.
2. In a small bowl, whisk together olive oil, lime juice, garlic, cumin, salt, and pepper.
3. Pour the dressing over the salad and toss until evenly coated.
4. Serve chilled or at room temperature.

Nutrition information per serving (serves 4):

Calories: 232 Total fat: 14g Saturated fat: 4g Carbohydrates: 21g Fiber: 7g Sugar: 4g Protein: 9g.

CHICKEN CAESAR WRAP

Total time: 15 minutes
Servings: 2

Ingredients:

- 1 large whole wheat tortilla wrap
- 4 oz sliced cooked chicken breast
- 2 tbsp Caesar dressing
- 1/4 cup diced cucumber
- 1/4 cup diced tomato
- 1/4 cup shredded Parmesan cheese
- 1/4 cup chopped fresh parsley
- Salt and pepper to taste

Directions:

1. Lay the tortilla wrap flat on a work surface.
2. Spread the Caesar dressing evenly over the tortilla, leaving a 1-inch border around the edges.
3. Layer the cooked chicken, cucumber, tomato, Parmesan cheese, and parsley over the dressing.
4. Season with salt and pepper to taste.
5. Roll the tortilla tightly, tucking in the ends as you go, to create a wrap.
6. Cut the wrap in half diagonally and serve.

Nutritional Information (per serving):

Calories: 329 Total Fat: 14g Saturated Fat: 4g Carbohydrates: 24g Fiber: 5g Sugar: 3g Protein: 27g.

CHAPTER 3 : SNACK AND APPETIZER

SPICY LENTIL BALLS

Total time: 35 minutes
Servings: 4

Ingredients:

- 1 can cooked lentils, drained and rinsed
- 1/2 cup shelled sunflower seeds
- 1/4 cup almond flour
- 1/2 teaspoon sea salt
- 1/2 teaspoon black pepper
- 1/2 teaspoon smoked paprika
- 1/2 teaspoon cayenne pepper

Instructions:

1. Preheat your oven to 375°F (190°C).
2. In a food processor, pulse the cooked lentils, sunflower seeds, almond flour, sea salt, black pepper, smoked paprika and cayenne pepper until the mixture forms a paste.
3. Using your hands, form the mixture into small balls or bite-sized squares.
4. Place the balls on a baking sheet lined with parchment paper.
5. Bake the bites for 15-20 minutes, or until lightly toasted.
6. Remove the bites from the oven and let them cool on the baking sheet for 5 minutes before serving.

Nutritional Information (per serving, 3 balls):

Calories: 180 Total Fat: 13g Saturated Fat: 1g Total Carbohydrates: 10g Sugars: 1g Protein: 8g

GARLIC ROASTED CAULIFLOWER

Total time: 35 minutes

Servings: 4

Ingredients:

- 1 head of cauliflower, chopped into florets
- 4 cloves garlic, minced
- 2 tablespoons olive oil
- 1/2 teaspoon salt
- 1/4 teaspoon black pepper

Instructions:

1. Preheat your oven to 425°F (218°C).
2. Line a baking sheet with parchment paper.
3. In a large bowl, toss the cauliflower florets with minced garlic, olive oil, salt, and black pepper until well coated.
4. Spread the cauliflower out onto the lined baking sheet.
5. Roast the cauliflower in the oven for 20-25 minutes, or until tender and slightly browned.
6. Serve the Garlic Roasted Cauliflower hot and enjoy!

Nutritional information (per serving, based on 4 servings):

Calories: 76 Total Fat: 5g Saturated Fat: 1g Total Carbohydrates: 7g Sugars: 3g Protein: 2g

MUSHROOM THYME SOUP

Total time: 35 minutes

Servings: 4

Ingredients:

- 1 tablespoon olive oil
- 1 medium onion, chopped
- 1 lb. mushrooms, chopped
- 2 cloves garlic, minced
- 1 tablespoon fresh thyme, chopped
- 4 cups vegetable broth
- 1/2 teaspoon dried oregano
- 1/2 teaspoon dried basil
- 1/2 teaspoon dried rosemary
- Salt and black pepper to taste
- Fresh parsley, chopped (optional)

Instructions:

1. Heat the olive oil in a large pot over medium heat.
2. Add the onion and cook for 2-3 minutes, or until translucent.
3. Add the chopped mushrooms, minced garlic, and chopped thyme to the pot and cook for an additional 5 minutes, stirring occasionally.
4. Add the vegetable broth, dried oregano, dried basil, and dried rosemary to the pot and bring to a boil.
5. Reduce the heat to low and simmer for 20-25 minutes, or until the mushrooms are tender.
6. Remove the pot from the heat and let it cool for a few minutes.
7. Use an immersion blender to puree the soup until smooth.
8. Season with salt and black pepper to taste.
9. Serve the Mushroom Thyme Soup hot, garnished with chopped parsley if desired.

Nutritional information (per serving, based on 4 servings):

Calories: 71 Total Fat: 4g Saturated Fat: 1g Total Carbohydrates: 8g Sugars: 4g Protein: 2g

CHOCOLATE CHIP BANANA BREAD

Total time: 60 minutes
Yield: 1 loaf

Ingredients:

- 2 ripe bananas, mashed
- 1/2 cup unsalted butter, melted
- 1/2 cup brown sugar
- 1/4 cup granulated sugar
- 2 eggs
- 1 teaspoon vanilla extract
- 1 1/2 cups all-purpose flour
- 1/2 teaspoon baking soda
- 1/2 teaspoon baking powder
- 1/4 teaspoon salt
- 1/2 cup chocolate chips

Instructions:

1. Preheat your oven to 350°F (175°C) and grease a loaf pan.
2. In a large bowl, whisk together the mashed bananas, melted butter, brown sugar, and granulated sugar until well combined.
3. Add the eggs and vanilla extract and whisk until well combined.
4. In a separate bowl, whisk together the all-purpose flour, baking soda, baking powder, and salt.
5. Gradually add the dry ingredients to the wet ingredients, stirring until just combined.
6. Fold in the chocolate chips.
7. Pour the batter into the prepared loaf pan and smooth out the top with a spatula.
8. Bake for 45-50 minutes, or until a toothpick inserted into the center comes out clean.
9. Remove the loaf pan from the oven and let the bread cool in the pan for a few minutes before transferring it to a wire rack to cool completely.
10. Slice and serve the Chocolate Chip Banana Bread and enjoy!

Nutritional information (per slice, based on 12 slices):

Calories: 229 Total Fat: 10g Saturated Fat: 6g Total Carbohydrates: 33g Sugars: 20g Protein: 3g

STRAWBERRY COCONUT CHIA PUDDING

Total time: 10 minutes (plus refrigeration time) Yield: 1 serving

Ingredients:

- 1/2 cup coconut milk
- 2 tablespoons chia seeds
- 1 tablespoon honey
- 1/2 teaspoon vanilla extract
- 1/4 teaspoon ground cinnamon
- 1/4 cup diced strawberries
- 1 tablespoon shredded coconut

Instructions:

1. In a small bowl, whisk together the coconut milk, chia seeds, honey, vanilla extract, and ground cinnamon.
2. Stir in the diced strawberries and shredded coconut.
3. Cover the bowl with plastic wrap or a lid and refrigerate for at least 2 hours or overnight.
4. Give the mixture a stir before serving and enjoy your Strawberry Coconut Chia Pudding!

Nutritional information (per serving):

Calories: 250 Total Fat: 19g Saturated Fat: 14g Total Carbohydrates: 18g Sugars: 12g Protein: 4g

CHAPTER 4 : DINNER

BEEF TACO BOWLS

Total time: 45 minutes
Yield: 4 servings

Ingredients:

- 1 cup quinoa
- 2 cups water
- 1 pound ground beef
- 2 teaspoons chili powder
- 1 teaspoon cumin
- Salt and pepper, to taste
- 1 red bell pepper, sliced
- 1 green bell pepper, sliced
- 1 onion, sliced
- 2 cloves garlic, minced
- 2 tablespoons olive oil
- Salsa, for topping
- Sour cream, for topping

Instructions:

1. Cook the quinoa according to package instructions.
2. In a small bowl, mix together the chili powder, cumin, salt, and pepper.
3. Add the ground beef to a large skillet over medium-high heat and cook until browned.
4. Drain the excess fat from the skillet and then add the spice mixture to the beef, stirring well to combine.
5. Add the sliced bell peppers, onion, and minced garlic to the skillet with the beef.
6. Cook for an additional 5-7 minutes, or until the vegetables are tender.
7. Divide the cooked quinoa among four bowls.
8. Top each bowl with the beef and vegetable mixture.
9. Serve the Beef Taco Bowls with salsa and a dollop of sour cream on top.

Nutritional information (per serving):

Calories: 487 Total Fat: 23g Saturated Fat: 7g Total Carbohydrates: 43g Sugars: 5g Protein: 29g

ONE PAN TURKEY TETRAZZINI

Total Time: 40 minutes

Yield: 6 servings

Ingredients:

- 1 pound ground turkey
- 1 onion, chopped
- 3 cloves garlic, minced
- 2 cups chicken broth
- 1 can diced tomatoes
- 1 can tomato sauce
- 1 teaspoon dried thyme
- 1 teaspoon dried oregano
- Salt and pepper, to taste
- 2 cups uncooked fusilli pasta
- 1 cup shredded mozzarella cheese
- Chopped fresh basil, for topping

Instructions:

1. In a large pan or skillet, cook the ground turkey over medium heat until browned.
2. Add the chopped onion and minced garlic to the pan and cook until softened, about 3-4 minutes.
3. Add the chicken broth, diced tomatoes, tomato sauce, thyme, oregano, salt, and pepper to the pan. Stir to combine.
4. Bring the mixture to a boil, then reduce the heat to low and cover the pan.
5. Simmer for 15-20 minutes, or until the sauce has thickened slightly.
6. Add the uncooked fusilli pasta to the pan and stir to combine.
7. Cover the pan and cook for an additional 10-12 minutes, or until the pasta is tender and the sauce has thickened.
8. Remove the pan from the heat and sprinkle the shredded mozzarella cheese over the top.
9. Cover the pan for a minute or two until the cheese is melted.
10. Serve the One Pan Turkey Tetrazzini with chopped fresh basil on top.

Nutritional information (per serving):

Calories: 385 Total Fat: 12g Saturated Fat: 4g Total Carbohydrates: 39g Sugars: 6g Protein: 30g

CILANTRO-LIME SHRIMP

Total time: 25 minutes

Yield: 4 servings

Ingredients:

- 1 pound large shrimp, peeled and deveined
- 1/2 cup cornmeal
- 1/4 cup breadcrumbs (gluten-free, if desired)
- 1 tablespoon chopped fresh cilantro
- 1 tablespoon chopped fresh lime zest
- 1 tablespoon olive oil
- 1 tablespoon lime juice
- Salt and pepper, to taste

Instructions:

1. Preheat the oven to 400°F (200°C). Line a baking sheet with parchment paper.
2. In a small bowl, mix together the cornmeal, breadcrumbs, cilantro, lime zest, salt, and pepper.
3. In another small bowl, whisk together the olive oil and lime juice.
4. Brush the top of each shrimp with the olive oil and lime juice mixture.
5. Press the cornmeal mixture onto the top of each shrimp, making sure to coat the entire surface.
6. Heat the olive oil in a large oven-safe skillet over medium-high heat.
7. Add the shrimp to the skillet, cornmeal-side down. Cook for 2-3 minutes, or until golden brown.
8. Carefully flip the shrimp over and transfer the skillet to the preheated oven.
9. Bake for 8-10 minutes, or until the shrimp is cooked through and pink.
10. Serve the Cilantro-Lime Shrimp immediately.

Nutritional information (per serving):

Calories: 210 Total Fat: 6g Saturated Fat: 1g Total Carbohydrates: 11g Sugars: 0g Protein: 27g

MUSHROOM AND SPINACH TORTELLINI

Total time: 25 minutes
Yield: 4 servings

Ingredients:

- 1 lb mushroom and spinach tortellini
- 1 tablespoon olive oil
- 1/2 cup sliced mushrooms
- 2 cups fresh spinach leaves
- 2 cloves garlic, minced
- 1/4 cup sliced black olives
- 1/4 cup chopped fresh parsley
- 1/4 cup grated Parmesan cheese
- Salt and pepper, to taste

Instructions:

1. Cook the mushroom and spinach tortellini according to package directions.
2. While the tortellini is cooking, heat the olive oil in a large skillet over medium heat.
3. Add the sliced mushrooms, fresh spinach leaves, and garlic to the skillet. Cook for 2-3 minutes, or until the mushrooms are tender and the spinach has wilted.
4. Add the sliced black olives to the skillet and cook for an additional 1-2 minutes.
5. Drain the cooked tortellini and add it to the skillet with the mushroom and spinach mixture. Toss to combine.
6. Stir in the chopped fresh parsley and grated Parmesan cheese. Season with salt and pepper to taste.
7. Serve the Mushroom and Spinach Tortellini immediately.

Nutritional information (per serving):

Calories: 390 Total Fat: 10g Saturated Fat: 3g Total Carbohydrates: 62g Sugars: 3g Protein: 16g

CREAMY VEGAN PUMPKIN RISOTTO

Total time: 45 minutes

Yield: 4 servings

Ingredients:

- 1 tablespoon olive oil
- 1 medium onion, chopped
- 3 cloves garlic, minced
- 1 1/2 cups Arborio rice
- 1/2 cup dry white wine
- 4 cups vegetable broth
- 1 small pumpkin, peeled and diced
- 1 teaspoon dried sage
- Salt and black pepper, to taste
- 1/4 cup nutritional yeast

Instructions:

1. Heat the olive oil in a large skillet over medium heat. Add the chopped onion and cook for 3-4 minutes, or until softened.
2. Add the minced garlic to the skillet and cook for an additional 1-2 minutes.
3. Add the Arborio rice to the skillet and stir to coat in the oil. Cook for 1-2 minutes, or until the rice is slightly toasted.
4. Pour in the dry white wine and stir continuously until the liquid is absorbed.
5. Gradually add the vegetable broth, 1 cup at a time, stirring continuously and allowing the liquid to be absorbed before adding more.
6. Add the diced pumpkin and dried sage to the skillet with the rice. Cook for an additional 15-20 minutes, or until the rice and pumpkin are tender and the risotto is creamy.
7. Season the risotto with salt and black pepper to taste. Stir in the nutritional yeast.
8. Serve the Creamy Vegan Pumpkin Risotto immediately, garnished with additional nutritional yeast and fresh herbs if desired.

Nutritional information (per serving):

Calories: 369 Total Fat: 6g Saturated Fat: 1g Total Carbohydrates: 69g Sugars: 4g Protein: 8g

VEGAN CHICKPEA COCONUT CURRY

Total time: 30 minutes

Yield: 4 servings

Ingredients:

- 1 tablespoon coconut oil
- 1 onion, diced
- 3 garlic cloves, minced
- 1 tablespoon grated ginger
- 1 red bell pepper, diced
- 2 tablespoons curry powder
- 1 can (14 ounces) coconut milk
- 1 can (14 ounces) chickpeas, drained and rinsed
- 1 cup vegetable broth
- 2 cups chopped spinach
- Salt and black pepper, to taste
- Juice of 1 lime
- Cooked rice or naan bread, for serving

Instructions:

1. Heat the coconut oil in a large skillet over medium heat. Add the diced onion and cook for 3-4 minutes, or until softened.
2. Add the minced garlic and grated ginger to the skillet and cook for an additional 1-2 minutes.
3. Add the diced red bell pepper to the skillet and cook for 2-3 minutes, or until slightly softened.
4. Add the curry powder to the skillet and stir to coat the vegetables. Cook for an additional 1-2 minutes, or until fragrant.
5. Pour in the coconut milk, chickpeas, and vegetable broth. Stir to combine and bring the mixture to a simmer.
6. Add the chopped spinach to the skillet and cook for an additional 3-4 minutes, or until wilted.
7. Season the curry with salt and black pepper to taste. Stir in the lime juice.

8. Serve the Vegan Chickpea Coconut Curry over cooked rice or with naan bread.

Nutritional information (per serving):

Calories: 355 Total Fat: 20g Saturated Fat: 15g Total Carbohydrates: 36g Sugars: 8g Protein: 9g

PLANT-BASED QUINOA AND BLACK BEAN BOWL

Total time: 30 minutes

Yield: 4 servings

Ingredients:

- 1 cup quinoa
- 1 can (15 ounces) black beans, drained and rinsed
- 1 red bell pepper, diced
- 1 yellow bell pepper, diced
- 1 small red onion, diced
- 1 avocado, diced
- 1/2 cup frozen corn, thawed
- 1/4 cup chopped fresh parsley
- 1 tablespoon olive oil
- 1 tablespoon chili powder
- 1 teaspoon ground cumin
- 1/2 teaspoon garlic powder
- Salt and black pepper, to taste
- Lime wedges, for serving

Instructions:

1. Cook the quinoa according to package instructions.
2. In a large skillet, heat the olive oil over medium heat. Add the diced red bell pepper, yellow bell pepper, and red onion to the skillet and cook for 3-4 minutes, or until slightly softened.
3. Add the chili powder, ground cumin, garlic powder, salt, and black pepper to the skillet. Stir to coat the vegetables in the spices.
4. Add the drained and rinsed black beans and thawed corn to the skillet. Cook for an additional 2-3 minutes, or until heated through.
5. To assemble the Plant-Based Quinoa and Black Bean Bowls, divide the cooked quinoa between 4 bowls. Top each bowl with the black bean and vegetable mixture. Add diced avocado and chopped parsley on top of each bowl.
6. Serve with lime wedges on the side.

Nutritional information (per serving):

Calories: 347 Total Fat: 12g Saturated Fat: 2g Total Carbohydrates: 51g Sugars: 4g Protein: 12g

ROASTED SWEET POTATO AND BROWN RICE BOWLS WITH BLACK BEANS

Ingredients:

- 2 medium sweet potatoes, scrubbed and cubed
- 1 tablespoon olive oil
- 1 teaspoon smoked paprika
- 1/2 teaspoon garlic powder
- Salt and pepper to taste
- 1 can black beans, drained and rinsed
- 1 cup cooked brown rice
- 1 avocado, sliced
- 1 lime, cut into wedges
- Fresh parsley, chopped (optional)

Instructions:

1. Preheat oven to 400°F (200°C).
2. In a large bowl, toss the cubed sweet potatoes with olive oil, smoked paprika, garlic powder, salt, and pepper.
3. Spread the seasoned sweet potatoes in a single layer on a baking sheet and roast for 20-25 minutes, or until tender and lightly browned.
4. In a separate bowl, mix together the black beans and brown rice.
5. To assemble the bowls, divide the roasted sweet potatoes and brown rice mixture equally among 4 bowls. Top each bowl with sliced avocado, a squeeze of lime juice, and fresh parsley, if desired.
6. Serve immediately and enjoy!

Nutritional Information per Serving:

Calories 370; Total Fats 13g; Saturated Fat 2g; Carbohydrate 54g; Sugar 8g; Fiber 13g; Protein 11g.

GREEK CHICKEN AND BROWN RICE BOWLS

Total Time: 35 minutes
Servings: 4

Ingredients:

- For the chicken:
- 4 boneless, skinless chicken breasts
- 1 tablespoon olive oil
- 1 tablespoon lemon juice
- 1 tablespoon dried oregano
- 1 teaspoon garlic powder
- Salt and pepper, to taste
- For the bowl:
- 2 cups cooked brown rice
- 1 can chickpeas, drained and rinsed
- 1 large cucumber, diced
- 1 cup cherry tomatoes, halved
- 1/4 cup pitted Kalamata olives, sliced
- 1/4 cup crumbled feta cheese
- 2 tablespoons chopped fresh parsley
- 2 tablespoons chopped fresh mint

Instructions:

1. Preheat oven to 375°F (190°C). In a small bowl, whisk together olive oil, lemon juice, oregano, garlic powder, salt, and pepper. Rub the mixture onto the chicken breasts and place on a baking sheet. Bake the chicken for 20-25 minutes, or until cooked through.
2. While the chicken is cooking, prepare the rice according to package instructions.
3. In a large bowl, combine the cooked rice, chickpeas, cucumber, cherry tomatoes, olives, feta cheese, parsley, and mint.
4. Once the chicken is done, slice it into strips.

5. To assemble the bowls, divide the rice mixture among four bowls, top with sliced chicken, and drizzle with dressing.
6. Serve immediately and enjoy!

Nutritional Information per Serving (1/4 of the recipe):

Calories 537; Total Fat 28g; Saturated Fat 6g; Carbohydrate 43g; Sugar 4g; Fiber 7g; Protein 33g.

SPICY THAI CURRY CHICKEN

Total time: 40 minutes
Servings: 4

Ingredients:

- 1 tablespoon vegetable oil
- 2 garlic cloves, minced
- 1 tablespoon ginger, minced
- 1 stalk lemongrass, bruised and chopped
- 1 small red onion, chopped
- 2 cups chicken broth
- 1 can coconut milk
- 1 tablespoon fish sauce
- 1 tablespoon honey
- 1 tablespoon lime juice
- 1 red bell pepper, thinly sliced
- 1 jalapeño pepper, thinly sliced
- 2 cups mixed vegetables (broccoli florets, carrots, and green beans), sliced
- 1 pound skinless, boneless chicken breasts, cubed
- Fresh basil leaves, for serving

Instructions:

1. In a large pot, heat the vegetable oil over medium heat. Add garlic, ginger, lemongrass, and red onion. Cook until fragrant, about 2-3 minutes.
2. Add the chicken broth, coconut milk, fish sauce, honey, and lime juice. Bring to a boil, then reduce heat and let simmer for 10-15 minutes.
3. Add the sliced bell pepper, jalapeño pepper, mixed vegetables, and chicken. Simmer for an additional 10-15 minutes, or until the chicken is cooked through.
4. Serve hot with fresh basil leaves on top. Enjoy!

Nutritional Information Per Serving (1/4 of the recipe):

Calories: 394 Total Fat: 22g Saturated Fat: 17g Total Carbohydrate: 18g Total Sugars: 11g Protein: 31g

CREAMY ROASTED TOMATO BASIL SOUP

Servings: 4
Total Time: 45 minutes

Ingredients:

- 3 lbs Roma tomatoes, halved
- 2 tablespoons olive oil
- 1 large onion, chopped
- 4 garlic cloves, minced
- 2 cups vegetable broth
- 2 tablespoons tomato paste
- 1/4 cup fresh basil leaves, chopped
- Salt and pepper to taste
- 1/4 cup heavy cream (optional)

Instructions:

1. Preheat oven to 400°F (200°C).
2. Place halved tomatoes on a baking sheet and drizzle with olive oil. Roast in the oven for 20-25 minutes or until the tomatoes are tender and slightly browned.
3. Heat olive oil in a large pot over medium heat. Add onion and garlic, cooking until onion is translucent.
4. Add roasted tomatoes, vegetable broth, and tomato paste to the pot. Bring to a simmer and let cook for 15-20 minutes.
5. Use an immersion blender to puree the soup until smooth. If you don't have an immersion blender, carefully transfer the soup to a blender and blend until smooth.
6. Stir in chopped basil and season with salt and pepper to taste.
7. Optional: Stir in heavy cream to create a creamier soup.
8. Serve hot and enjoy!

Nutritional Information Per Serving (1/4 of recipe):

Calories: 194 Total Fat: 11g Saturated Fat: 3g Carbohydrate: 22g Sugar: 13g Fiber: 5g Protein: 4g

MEDITERRANEAN BAKED COD WITH COLORFUL VEGETABLES

Servings: 4
Total Time: Approximately 30 minutes

Ingredients:

- 4 cod fillets
- 1 red onion, chopped
- 2 bell peppers, sliced
- 2 zucchinis, sliced
- 1 cup cherry tomatoes
- 3 cloves garlic, minced
- 2 tablespoons olive oil
- 1 tablespoon lemon juice
- 1 teaspoon dried oregano
- Salt and pepper to taste

Instructions:

1. Preheat the oven to 400°F (200°C).
2. Place the cod fillets in a large baking dish.
3. In a separate bowl, combine the chopped onion, sliced bell peppers, sliced zucchinis, cherry tomatoes, minced garlic, olive oil, lemon juice, dried oregano, salt, and pepper. Mix well to coat the vegetables.
4. Pour the vegetable mixture evenly over the cod fillets in the baking dish.
5. Bake for 20-25 minutes, or until the cod is cooked through and flakes easily with a fork, and the vegetables are tender.
6. Remove from the oven and serve hot.

Nutritional Information per Serving (1 fillet with vegetables):

Calories: 260 Total Fat: 8g Saturated Fat: 1.5g Carbohydrates: 11g Sugar: 6g Fiber: 3g Protein: 38g

SAVORY MUSHROOM AND SPINACH PIZZA

Total Time: 25 minutes
Servings: 4

Ingredients:

- 1 pizza crust (homemade or store-bought)
- 1/4 cup pizza sauce
- 1/2 cup sliced mushrooms
- 1 cup baby spinach leaves
- 1/2 cup shredded mozzarella cheese
- 1/4 cup crumbled feta cheese
- 1 tablespoon olive oil
- Salt and pepper to taste

Instructions:

1. Preheat the oven to 425°F (220°C).
2. Place the pizza crust on a baking sheet or pizza stone.
3. Spread the pizza sauce evenly over the crust.
4. Arrange the sliced mushrooms and baby spinach leaves on top of the sauce.
5. Sprinkle the shredded mozzarella cheese and crumbled feta cheese over the vegetables.
6. Drizzle the olive oil over the top and season with salt and pepper.
7. Bake in the preheated oven for 12-15 minutes or until the crust is golden brown and the cheese is melted.
8. Slice the pizza and serve it hot.

Nutritional Information per Serving (1/4 of pizza):

Calories: 300 Total Fat: 13g Saturated Fat: 5g Carbohydrate: 30g Sugar: 2g Fiber: 2g Protein: 12g

MUSHROOM AND SPINACH ALFREDO PASTA

Servings: 4
Total Time: 30-35 minutes

Ingredients:

- 8 oz. fettuccine pasta
- 2 tbsp olive oil
- 8 oz. mushrooms, sliced
- 3 cloves garlic, minced
- 4 cups fresh baby spinach
- 1 cup heavy cream
- 1/2 cup grated Parmesan cheese
- Salt and black pepper, to taste

Instructions:

1. Cook fettuccine according to package directions. Drain and set aside.
2. Heat olive oil in a large skillet over medium-high heat.
3. Add sliced mushrooms and garlic. Sauté until the mushrooms are browned and tender, about 5 minutes.
4. Add fresh baby spinach and continue to cook until wilted, about 1-2 minutes.
5. Add heavy cream and bring to a simmer. Simmer for 2-3 minutes until the sauce is slightly thickened.
6. Add cooked fettuccine pasta to the skillet and toss to coat with the sauce.
7. Add grated Parmesan cheese and continue to toss until the cheese is melted and the pasta is fully coated.
8. Season with salt and black pepper, to taste.
9. Serve hot and enjoy!

Nutritional Information (per serving):

Calories: 540 Total Fat: 34g Saturated Fat: 18g Total Carbohydrate: 42g Total Sugars: 3g Protein: 19g

SPICY VEGETABLE FRIED RICE

Total Time: 20 minutes
Servings: 4

Ingredients:

- 2 cups cooked brown rice, chilled
- 1/2 cup crumbled firm tofu
- 2 tablespoons vegetable oil
- 1 small onion 1, chopped
- 1 zucchini, chopped
- 1 red bell pepper, chopped
- 1 jalapeño pepper, chopped
- 2 garlic cloves, minced
- 1 tablespoon grated fresh ginger
- 1 tablespoon soy sauce
- 1 tablespoon hoisin sauce
- 1/2 teaspoon red pepper flakes
- 2 green onions, chopped
- Salt and pepper to taste

Instructions:

1. Heat 1 tablespoon of vegetable oil in a large skillet over high heat.
2. Add crumbled tofu and stir-fry for 2-3 minutes until slightly crispy. Remove tofu from skillet and set aside.
3. Add another tablespoon of vegetable oil to the same skillet. Add onion, zucchini, red bell pepper, jalapeño pepper, garlic, and ginger, and stir-fry for 3-4 minutes until vegetables are tender.
4. Add cooked rice to the skillet and stir-fry for 2-3 minutes until the rice is heated through.
5. Add soy sauce, hoisin sauce, red pepper flakes, and stir to combine.
6. Add the cooked tofu back to the skillet and stir-fry for 1-2 minutes until everything is evenly coated.
7. Season with salt and pepper to taste.

8. Garnish with chopped green onions and serve hot.

Nutritional Information (per serving):

Calories: 290 Total Fat: 13g Saturated Fat: 1g Total Carbohydrate: 34g Total Sugars: 8g Protein: 9g

CHAPTER 5 : DESSERT

CHOCOLATE AND ORANGE OLIVE OIL CAKE

Servings: 8
Total Time: 50 minutes

Ingredients:

- 1 and 1/2 cups all-purpose flour
- 1/2 cup unsweetened cocoa powder
- 1 tsp baking powder
- 1/4 tsp salt
- 3/4 cup granulated sugar
- 1/2 cup extra-virgin olive oil
- 2 large eggs
- 1 tbsp orange zest
- 1 tsp vanilla extract
- 1/2 cup freshly squeezed orange juice
- Confectioner's sugar for dusting

Instructions:

1. Preheat the oven to 350°F (175°C) and grease a 9-inch round cake pan with olive oil.
2. In a medium bowl, whisk together the flour, cocoa powder, baking powder, and salt until well combined.
3. In a large bowl, whisk together the granulated sugar and olive oil until light and fluffy, and then add in the eggs one at a time, whisking well between additions.
4. Stir in the orange zest and vanilla extract.
5. Fold in the dry mixture to the wet mixture, alternating with the orange juice, until just combined.
6. Pour the batter into the prepared cake pan and bake for 30-35 minutes or until a toothpick inserted in the center comes out clean.
7. Once done, let the cake cool in the pan for 10 minutes, then transfer it to a wire rack to cool completely.
8. Dust the top of the cake with confectioner's sugar before serving.

Nutritional Information (per serving):

Calories: 260 Total Fat: 12g Saturated Fat: 2g Total Carbohydrate: 35g Total Sugars: 20g Protein: 3g

BLUEBERRY ALMOND OATMEAL PANCAKES

Servings: 4
Total time: 25 minutes

Ingredients:

- 1 and 1/2 cups rolled oats
- 1 cup unsweetened almond milk
- 2 large eggs
- 1/2 cup almond flour
- 1/4 cup maple syrup
- 1 tsp baking powder
- 1/2 tsp ground cinnamon
- 1/4 tsp salt
- 1/2 cup fresh blueberries
- 2 tbsp sliced almonds

Instructions:

1. In a blender or food processor, blend the rolled oats until they become a fine powder.
2. In a large bowl, whisk together the blended oats, almond milk, eggs, almond flour, maple syrup, baking powder, cinnamon, and salt until smooth.
3. Fold in the blueberries and sliced almonds.
4. Heat a nonstick pan over medium heat. Once hot, pour the batter onto the pan using a 1/4 cup measuring cup.
5. Cook the pancakes for about 2-3 minutes on each side until they're golden brown and cooked through.
6. Serve with additional blueberries and sliced almonds on top, and a drizzle of maple syrup if desired.

Nutritional Information (per serving):

Calories: 350 Total Fat: 15g Saturated Fat: 1.5g Total Carbohydrate: 44g Total Sugars: 16g Protein: 12g

CLASSIC TIRAMISU

Prep Time: 30 minutes Chill Time: 2 hours or overnight
Servings: 12

Ingredients:

- 6 egg yolks
- 3/4 cup granulated sugar
- 2/3 cup whole milk
- 1 1/4 cups heavy cream
- 1/2 tsp vanilla extract
- 1 lb mascarpone cheese
- 1/2 cup strong espresso, cooled
- 1/4 cup amaretto liqueur
- 24 ladyfingers
- Unsweetened cocoa powder, for dusting

Instructions:

1. Whisk egg yolks and sugar until creamy.
2. Heat milk until steaming; add to egg mixture.
3. Cook mixture until thickened; let it cool.
4. Beat heavy cream and vanilla until stiff peaks form.
5. Beat mascarpone until smooth; fold in whipped cream.
6. Mix espresso and amaretto in a small bowl.
7. Dip ladyfingers in espresso mixture and arrange in a baking dish.
8. Spread half of the mascarpone mixture over the ladyfingers.
9. Repeat with another layer of soaked ladyfingers and mascarpone mixture.
10. Refrigerate for 2 hours or overnight.
11. Dust with cocoa powder before serving.

Nutritional Information (per serving):

Calories: 460 Total Fat: 36g Saturated Fat: 21g Total Carbohydrate: 24g Total Sugars: 18g
Protein: 7g

BLUEBERRY OATMEAL MUFFINS

Prep Time: 35 minutes
Servings: 12

Ingredients:

- 1 and 1/2 cups all-purpose flour
- 1 cup rolled oats
- 1/2 cup granulated sugar
- 2 tsp baking powder
- 1/2 tsp baking soda
- 1/2 tsp salt
- 1 cup unsweetened almond milk
- 1/4 cup vegetable oil
- 2 large eggs
- 1 tsp vanilla extract
- 1 cup fresh blueberries

Instructions:

1. Preheat your oven to 400°F (200°C). Grease a 12-cup muffin tin or line with muffin cups.
2. In a large mixing bowl, whisk together the all-purpose flour, rolled oats, granulated sugar, baking powder, baking soda, and salt.
3. In a separate bowl, whisk together the almond milk, vegetable oil, eggs, and vanilla extract.
4. Add the wet ingredients to the dry ingredients and mix until just combined.
5. Fold in the blueberries.
6. Fill each muffin cup about 3/4 full with batter.
7. Bake for 18-20 minutes or until a toothpick inserted in the center comes out clean.
8. Let the muffins cool in the pan for 5 minutes before transferring to a wire rack to cool completely.

Nutritional Information (per muffin):

Calories: 180 Total Fat: 6g Saturated Fat: 1g Total Carbohydrate: 28g Total Sugars: 10g Protein: 4g

RASPBERRY LEMON MUFFINS

Prep Time: 35 minutes
Servings: 12

Ingredients:

- 1 and 3/4 cups all-purpose flour
- 1 teaspoon baking powder
- 1/2 teaspoon baking soda
- 1/4 teaspoon salt
- 1/2 cup unsalted butter, softened
- 3/4 cup granulated sugar
- 2 large eggs
- 1 teaspoon vanilla extract
- 1/2 cup fresh raspberries
- 1 tablespoon lemon zest
- Juice of 1/2 lemon

Instructions:

1. Preheat oven to 350°F (180°C). Line a muffin tin with muffin liners.
2. In a medium bowl, whisk together flour, baking powder, baking soda, and salt.
3. In a large bowl, cream butter and sugar together until light and fluffy.
4. Beat in eggs one at a time, then stir in vanilla extract, lemon zest and lemon juice.
5. Mix in fresh raspberries.
6. Gradually mix in the dry ingredients until just combined.
7. Divide the batter evenly among the muffin cups, filling each about 2/3 full.
8. Bake for 18-20 minutes or until a toothpick inserted in the center comes out clean.
9. Let the muffins cool in the pan for 5 minutes before transferring to a wire rack to cool completely.

Nutrition Information (per serving):

Calories: 236 Total Fat: 11g Saturated Fat: 6.5g Total Carbohydrate: 31g Total Sugars: 15g Protein: 3.5g

BLUEBERRY OATMEAL PANCAKES

Total time: 20 minutes
Servings: 8

Ingredients:

- 1 cup all-purpose flour
- 1/2 cup rolled oats
- 1 tablespoon baking powder
- 1/2 teaspoon salt
- 1/4 cup brown sugar
- 1 cup milk
- 1 egg
- 2 tablespoons vegetable oil
- 1 teaspoon vanilla extract
- 1 cup fresh blueberries

Instructions:

1. Mix together flour, oats, baking powder, salt, and brown sugar in a mixing bowl.
2. In a separate bowl, whisk together the milk, egg, vegetable oil, and vanilla extract.
3. Add the wet mixture to the dry mixture and whisk until just combined (lumps are okay).
4. Gently fold in the fresh blueberries.
5. Heat a non-stick skillet or griddle over medium heat. Scoop 1/4 cup of batter onto the skillet for each pancake.
6. Cook until bubbles form on the surface of the pancake and the edges begin to look set, about 2-3 minutes. Flip and cook for another 1-2 minutes until golden brown.
7. Serve hot with butter, maple syrup, or whipped cream.

Nutritional Information (per serving):

Calories: 210 Total Fat: 7g Saturated Fat: 1g Total Carbohydrate: 32g Total Sugars: 11g Protein: 5g

BANANA WALNUT PANCAKES

Total time: 20 minutes
Servings: 8

Ingredients:

- 1 cup all-purpose flour
- 1 tbsp white sugar
- 2 tsp baking powder
- 1/2 tsp salt
- 1 cup milk
- 1 banana, mashed
- 1 egg
- 2 tbsp unsalted butter, melted
- 1/4 cup chopped walnuts

Instructions:

1. In a mixing bowl, combine the flour, sugar, baking powder, and salt.
2. In a separate bowl, whisk together the milk, mashed banana, egg, and melted butter.
3. Pour the wet mixture into the dry mixture and whisk until just combined (lumps are okay).
4. Gently fold in the chopped walnuts.
5. Heat a non-stick skillet over medium-high heat.
6. Pour 1/4 cup of the pancake batter onto the skillet for each pancake.
7. Cook for 2-3 minutes on each side or until golden brown.
8. Serve hot with your favorite toppings, such as sliced bananas, chopped walnuts, or a drizzle of honey.

Nutrition information (per serving):

Calories: 210 Total Fat: 9g Saturated Fat: 4g Total Carbohydrate: 28g Total Sugars: 8g Protein: 5g

BLUEBERRY LEMON CHIA SEED LOAF

Total Time: 1 hour 15 minutes
Servings: 10-12

Ingredients:

- 1 1/2 cups all-purpose flour
- 1/2 cup almond flour
- 1/2 cup chia seeds
- 2 teaspoons baking powder
- 1/2 teaspoon baking soda
- 1/2 teaspoon salt
- 1/2 cup unsalted butter, softened
- 3/4 cup granulated sugar
- 2 large eggs
- 1 teaspoon vanilla extract
- 1/2 cup plain Greek yogurt
- 1/4 cup fresh lemon juice
- 1 tablespoon grated lemon zest
- 1 cup fresh blueberries

Instructions:

1. Preheat the oven to 350°F. Grease a loaf pan and set aside.
2. In a medium bowl, whisk together the all-purpose flour, almond flour, chia seeds, baking powder, baking soda, and salt.
3. In a large bowl, cream together the butter and sugar until light and fluffy, about 3-4 minutes. Add the eggs, one at a time, mixing well after each addition. Stir in the vanilla extract, Greek yogurt, lemon juice, and lemon zest.
4. Gradually add the dry ingredients to the wet ingredients, mixing until just combined. Gently fold in the fresh blueberries.
5. Pour the batter into the prepared loaf pan and smooth the top. Bake for 45-50 minutes, or until a toothpick inserted into the center of the cake comes out clean.
6. Let the cake cool in the pan for 10 minutes before removing it from the pan and transferring it to a wire rack to cool completely.

7. Slice and serve the loaf as is or, if desired, dust with powdered sugar before serving.

Nutrition information:

Calories: 250 Fat: 14g Saturated Fat: 6g Carbohydrates: 27g Fiber: 5g Sugar: 11g Protein: 6g

PEANUT BUTTER OATMEAL CHOCOLATE CHIP COOKIES

Total Time: 30 minutes Servings: Approximately 20 cookies

Ingredients:

- 1/2 cup all-purpose flour
- 1 tsp baking powder
- 1/2 tsp baking soda
- 1/4 tsp salt
- 1/2 cup unsalted butter, room temperature
- 1/2 cup creamy peanut butter
- 1/2 cup granulated sugar
- 1/2 cup packed light brown sugar
- 1 large egg
- 1/2 tsp vanilla extract
- 1 1/2 cups old-fashioned oats
- 1 cup semisweet chocolate chips

Instructions:

1. Preheat the oven to 350°F (175°C) and line a baking sheet with parchment paper.
2. In a medium bowl, whisk together flour, baking powder, baking soda, and salt.
3. In a large bowl, use an electric mixer to beat the butter, peanut butter, granulated sugar, and brown sugar until creamy (about 2-3 minutes).
4. Beat in the egg and vanilla until well combined.
5. Gradually add the flour mixture, beating until just combined.
6. Stir in the oats and chocolate chips.
7. Using a cookie scoop or spoon, drop the dough onto the prepared baking sheet.
8. Bake for 12-15 minutes, or until the edges are lightly golden. Allow the cookies to cool on the baking sheet for 5 minutes before transferring them to a wire rack to cool completely.

Nutrition information:

Calories: 235 Total Fat: 12g Saturated Fat: 5g Total Carbohydrate: 29g Total Sugars: 19g
Protein: 4g

NO-BAKE GREEK YOGURT BERRY TART

Total time: 15 minutes (plus chilling time)
Servings: 8

Ingredients:

For the Crust:

- 1 cup almond flour
- 1/4 cup unsweetened shredded coconut
- 2 tablespoons coconut oil, melted
- 2 tablespoons honey or maple syrup

For the Filling:

- 1 1/2 cups Greek yogurt
- 2 tablespoons honey or maple syrup
- 1 teaspoon vanilla extract

For the Topping:

- Assorted fresh berries (such as strawberries, blueberries, raspberries)

Instructions:

1. In a mixing bowl, combine almond flour, shredded coconut, melted coconut oil, and honey (or maple syrup) for the crust. Stir until well combined and press the mixture into the bottom of a tart pan or pie dish to form the crust. Place it in the refrigerator to chill while preparing the filling.
2. In another bowl, whisk together Greek yogurt, honey (or maple syrup), and vanilla extract until smooth and well combined.
3. Remove the chilled crust from the refrigerator and spread the Greek yogurt mixture evenly over the crust.
4. Arrange the fresh berries on top of the Greek yogurt filling in an attractive pattern.
5. Place the tart in the refrigerator for at least 1 hour to set and chill.
6. Serve chilled and enjoy!

Nutritional Information (per serving):

Calories: 220 Total Fat: 15g Saturated Fat: 6g Total Carbohydrate: 17g Total Sugars: 10g Protein: 7g Fiber: 3g

Made in the USA
Las Vegas, NV
30 October 2023

79914417R00057